Made in the USA
Middletown, DE
15 October 2023

40807916R00056